THE EDGE of THE SKY
SHENANDOAH
—NATIONAL PARK ROAD GUIDE—

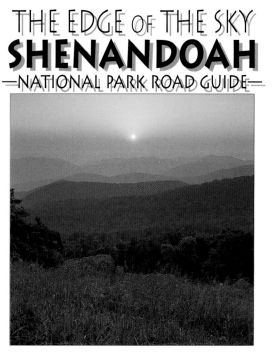

BY
ROSE HOUK

SIERRA PRESS
MARIPOSA, CA

ACKNOWLEDGMENTS

My first debt is to Jeff Nicholas of Sierra Press, who asked about my interest in writing a book on Shenandoah National Park. It took me about an instant to say yes, but then I realized how much I would need the help of others. I owe deep appreciation to many good Park Service folks for willing assistance and reviews of the manuscript—Reed Engle, Rolf Gubler, Karen Michaud, Claire Comer, and Mara Meisel—and to Greta Miller of the Shenandoah National Park Association. Dave Haskell and Ron Litwin also shared their valuable knowledge of the park. Nicky Leach did her usual superb editing job. And to Ellen and Dennis Ahr, I offer warmest gratitude for providing a welcome home away from home. And finally to Michael Collier, who keeps showing me new ways to see.
                                    —Rose Houk

INSIDE FRONT COVER
Blooming redbud bordering Skyline Drive.
PHOTO ©PAT & CHUCK BLACKLEY
PAGE 2
Skyline Drive. PHOTO ©PAT & CHUCK BLACKLEY
TITLE PAGE
Sunset seen from The Point.
PHOTO ©PAT & CHUCK BLACKLEY
ABOVE
Lower Doyles River Falls, spring.
PHOTO ©TERRY DONNELLY
OPPOSITE
Sunset, Hazeltop Ridge. PHOTO ©CHARLES GURCHE

CONTENTS

ABOVE
Sunset along the Blue Ridge.
PHOTO ©CHARLES GURCHE
OPPOSITE
Maples in autumn glory in an oak woodland.
PHOTO ©CARR CLIFTON

SHENANDOAH
AN INTRODUCTION

In September 2003, Hurricane Isabel whirled up the Atlantic coast and ripped a wide swath of destruction through the heart of Shenandoah. Gale-force winds uprooted brittle black locusts, splintered strong oaks, and occasionally toppled entire trees onto roads and roofs. The park was closed for a time as crews worked nonstop to clear thousands of downed trees in time for the promised throngs that would soon descend to view the fall colors.

My husband and I arrived two weeks after the hurricane, and autumn was just getting out the paints and brushes. A smattering of vines and trees was undergoing that miraculous transformation that takes place each year in the eastern deciduous forest. Virginia creeper streaked crimson across gray rocks along Skyline Drive. Hickories and black gums gleamed yellow and orange. Goldenrods and asters bloomed in the last corners of warmth. Polished brown acorns littered the trails, awaiting the mouths of voracious squirrels and birds and bears. Turkey vultures tilted effortlessly over the ridges, forming alliances for the long trip south for the winter. Monarch butterflies fluttered at purple thistles, sipping nectar to fuel their epic migration.

We spent our first night in the park at Mathews Arm Campground, happy to find it open. A cold front tumbled nighttime temperatures toward freezing, and we were forced to add a blanket to our camper bed. The brisk winds ushered in crystalline air that allowed stunning views of the surrounding terrain.

Long-distance vistas are among Shenandoah National Park's most treasured attributes—from high on the Skyline Drive, we gazed west to the Shenandoah River meandering gracefully through the Shenandoah Valley, backed by the stalwart line of Massanutten Mountain, and beyond to the indigo Alleghenies in West Virginia. At other overlooks, the aspect was eastward across the hills of the Piedmont rolling up from the coastal plain.

The drive, which stays to a lofty path through the park, affords easy access to the highest peaks. Most ask only a short hike to rocky summits rising nearly 4,000 feet above sea level. During our trip we also walked downhill, to waterfalls snugged deep in the woods like glistening jewels. We strolled through the dew-draped grasses of Big Meadows. And as we continued south down the drive, we sampled the three other campgrounds, finding at breezy Loft Mountain that we had to throw yet another blanket on the bed.

We explored more trails, saw more places that have impressed themselves in the hearts of those who know and love Shenandoah—Hightop, Hawksbill, Stony Man, Dark Hollow, South River, Jones Run, Marys Rock. I was becoming reacquainted with some of these places after a 25-year absence. A city dweller then, I was always eager to flee the sultry summers of Washington,

TOP
View into Shenandoah Valley.
PHOTO ©JEFF GNASS
MIDDLE
Upper Doyles River Falls.
PHOTO ©PAT & CHUCK BLACKLEY
BOTTOM
Colorful autumn leaves near Camp Hoover. PHOTO ©PAT & CHUCK BLACKLEY

OPPOSITE: Dogwood blossoms in the fog. PHOTO ©CHARLES GURCHE

D.C., happy to seek the good tidings that mountains invariably bring.

Despite the years that had passed, memories welled up on this post-hurricane trip. Certainly I recalled Big Meadows, its openness intriguing and refreshing amid the tight tangle of forest. There was the night spent in an old log cabin after a day of work on the Appalachian Trail. And the thrilling sight of a bobcat walking beside Jeremys Run near where I was camped, casting its wary eye upon the intruder. For that bobcat—and the bear, the deer, the birds, the trees, the shrubs, the fish, the snakes, the salamanders, and every other living thing—Shenandoah remains an essential refuge. Here, nature holds sway and displays unswerving resilience.

Later I learned that Shenandoah National Park was carved from the holdings of more than a thousand individual landowners. When the state of Virginia condemned land for the park-to-be, residents had to leave their homes so that anyone could visit these gentle woods. The word "sacrifice" may not overstate their departure.

So it seemed only appropriate at the end of another recent trip that I should pay a visit to an old home place, this time in the spring. From Dickey Ridge Visitor Center, I grabbed my walking stick for the loop walk through Fox Hollow. Thumb-sized tulip poplar petals sprinkled the trail, thick grape vines ribboned over the odd rock piles, and profuse white flowers festooned the multiflora rose. Generations of the Fox family lived on the farm here. They cleared fields, grew their food, canned cherries, churned butter, made sassafras tea, and probably savored the shade of the old spreading sycamore on hot summer days. They were born, married, and were buried here. Among the periwinkle and daisies stand the modest headstones of Lemuel F. Fox, "Aged 78 Years," and Gertrude Fox, only 21 when she died.

I am grateful to the Foxes and all the others who gave up their homes to the forest, its uncountable plants and animals, and the rhythms of the seasons—the quiet of winter, the joy of spring, the constant motion of summer, and the grand finale of autumn—to create a park for all people.

TOP
Autumn forest at dawn.
PHOTO ©MICHAEL J. HICKEY/PlacePhoto.com
ABOVE
Jones Run Falls.
PHOTO ©MICHAEL COLLIER

THE SHENANDOAH REGION

The Blue Ridge Mountains begin a sharp, steady rise in north-central Virginia, part of the greater Appalachian Mountain chain. Stretching 70 miles north to south, Shenandoah National Park forms a long, narrow bulwark of the Blue Ridge between the Piedmont to the east and the Shenandoah Valley to the west.

The leafy corridor of Skyline Drive sweeps down the spine of the park. Reaching heights of nearly 3,700 feet, the road provides the perfect platform for viewing the surrounding terrain. From many overlooks and pullouts along the way, Shenandoah's special geographical and topographical significance can be appreciated.

These old mountains stand high because they are made of resistant rock. Down their steep flanks, a hundred streams have hollowed out valleys and coves. To the east, the streams drain directly into the Potomac River, Chesapeake Bay, and the Atlantic Ocean. Only about 80 miles eastward, as the raven flies, sits the nation's capital. Once upon a time, it was said, the Washington Monument could be seen from the mountains. True or not, Shenandoah today indisputably draws millions of residents from the District of Columbia.

Dominating the view to the west is the long dark massif of Massanutten Mountain, in the George Washington National Forest. The prongs of the South and North Forks of the Shenandoah River cradle the mountain; as it flows north, the Shenandoah eventually stages a dramatic meeting with the Potomac at Harpers Ferry, West Virginia.

With a pleasing patchwork of bucolic farms and small towns, the Shenandoah Valley still presents a strongly rural character. On clear days, it's possible to see beyond the long blue line of "The Massanutten," as it's called, all the way to West Virginia's Allegheny Mountains.

For many thousands of years people have traveled in these mystical mountains. They still do, now two million or so each year, reveling in the woods and the waterfalls and relishing the relief from the hustle and humidity of the low country. Especially on weekends, visitors ascend to camp, walk, fish, or ride a horse; see a bear, a bird, or a flower; or just stretch the eyes and rest the mind.

TOP: Pre-dawn view from Ivy Creek Overlook. PHOTO ©MICHAEL J. HICKEY/PlacePhoto.com

THE APPALACHIAN TRAIL

In the early 20th century, Massachusetts forester Benton MacKaye proposed the Appalachian Trail with a simple motive in mind: "To walk. To see. And to see what you see."

Work on the "AT," as it's known, began in the 1920s. Through the efforts of volunteer labor, the path now extends for more than 2,100 miles through 14 states, from Mount Katahdin in Maine to Springer Mountain in Georgia. Shenandoah National Park claims 101 of those miles. The trail's highest elevation in the park—3,837 feet—is reached at an intersection with the Stony Man Trail near Skyland.

Now an official national scenic trail, the AT is marked everywhere with distinctive white blazes on trees. It first crosses the Skyline Drive at Compton Gap, Mile 10.4, and intersects the road 30 more times in the park. Hikers spend the night at conveniently located huts and shelters, or at cabins maintained by the Potomac Appalachian Trail Club. Club members, with the Park Service, maintain the trail through the park.

The lure and mystique of the Appalachian Trail are irresistible. People walk it for an hour, a day, a weekend, a week, or for months—three to four million of them a year, in fact.

A much smaller number, some 3,000 each year, are "through-hikers" who set out to complete the entire length. Fewer than one in six actually finish this ambitious task. One who was well on his way was a young man at Ivy Creek in Shenandoah. He decided to undertake the grand trek after he graduated from high school. It was October, and he and three friends were southbound, hoping to reach Springer Mountain by Thanksgiving. Carrying 38 pounds on his back, he was averaging 17 miles a day. One day, he and his companions completed 26 miles by walking day and night, something he didn't plan to repeat. So far, they'd seen no bears, only bothersome raccoons. Armed with two walking sticks, dressed in shorts, T-shirt, and knee-high gaiters, with radio earphones in his ears, the young man politely declined offers of food, saying he was well supplied. He kept in touch with his parents and girlfriend when he could.

Another through-hiker, a baby-boomer making his way up Hightop, sat on a boulder and took a breather. It was tough to have an uphill push at the end of a day in a drizzle, but he seemed perfectly happy to be just where he was. It wasn't his first AT hike. When asked why he undertakes the journey, his answer would likely have won Benton MacKaye's approval: "Because I like it," he said. "I just like walking in the woods in the fall."

ABOVE: The Appalachian Trail near Hogback Overlook. PHOTO ©PAT & CHUCK BLACKLEY   **OPPOSITE:** The Appalachian Trail and azaleas. PHOTO ©ED KING

GEOLOGIC HISTORY: GRANITES AND GREENSTONES

Mountains come and mountains go. In a nutshell, that is the geologic story of Shenandoah National Park. Of course that's a bit simplistic, not to mention a bit difficult to swallow.

Thoughts about mountains have changed. In past centuries, geologists suggested that the massive uplifts originated as wrinkles in our shrinking, cooling planet. More recently, those ideas were revolutionized by the discovery of continental drift, and on its heels plate tectonics—the notion that slabs of Earth's crust go scooting around the globe like bumper cars at the fair. The theory of plate tectonics, now well proven, is invoked to explain the existence not only of mountains but also oceans and most other major landforms.

The Appalachian Mountains of the eastern United States are no exception— they too are believed to be the result of such monumental movements. The Appalachians stretch nearly 2,000 miles from Newfoundland to Alabama. Their central and southern portions are known as the Blue Ridge Mountains, of which Shenandoah is part.

The Appalachians are among the oldest mountains in North America. The rock exposed in them dates to the dimmest period of geologic time, some one billion years past. Not only the rock that makes them but also the mountains themselves are grandfathers compared to young whippersnappers like the modern Rockies or Sierra Nevada in the West.

Three major mountain-building episodes, or orogenies, created the ancestral Appalachians. A fourth, and most recent, episode gave rise to the range we see today. During this time, about 330 million years ago, all the plates generally fused into a "montage" of megacontinents-called Pangaea. In this great unification, a soon-to-be Africa encountered North America in a chaotic collision. The edges of the two plates ground away at each other

over the ensuing 50 million years or so. As the African plate was forced down underneath North America, the land was compressed and elevated into very high mountains. Think of the Misty Mountains of Tolkien's Middle Earth, writes author Ron Redfern, and you've got the close idea of the Appalachians.

Such a cataclysm tends to fold, crack, or break rocks—sometimes on a small scale, sometimes on a much larger scale. The Appalachians have been so tortuously folded, faulted, refolded, and turned on their heads that reconstructing their geologic past requires some real sleuthing. Thanks to the painstaking work of geologists, we now know much more about the deep, fascinating history of these venerable mountains. Admittedly, geologists sometimes are challenged to get that closeup view in Shenandoah, furred with forest and frequently shrouded in fog. But on mountaintops, such as the craggy face of Stony Man or the sawtooth cliffs of Hawksbill, it's possible to gain that perspective. In roadcuts along Skyline Drive, rock is also beautifully exposed and easily examined.

The Blue Ridge Mountains of Shenandoah still tower above the surrounding valleys and the Piedmont because they are made of hard rocks. Unlike the softer, sedimentary rocks of the valleys, these hard rocks erode less readily. The oldest and toughest started out as "basement" rock. In Shenandoah, this is the Pedlar Formation, mostly quartz monzonite and gneiss, and the Old Rag Granite, which intruded the Pedlar. The Old Rag Granite is named for the mountain that stands in mysterious solitude east of the main range; it is best displayed there on the crest as smooth, rounded boulders, grayish-white and chocked full with a coarse-grained mosaic of blue quartz and large feldspar crystals.

A little younger, but only relatively, is the Catoctin Formation. This rock started life as lava and other volcanic material, probably produced when a precursor to the Atlantic Ocean was opening about 600 million years ago. Magma—rock

ABOVE: Granite boulder atop Old Rag Mountain. PHOTO ©CHARLES GURCHE

cooked beneath the earth's surface until it melts to a liquid—welled up along fractures and spilled over the nearly leveled terrain. A series of flows were laid up, and as they cooled they formed vertical columns in the shape of polygons. These columnar joints can be seen at Little Stony Man and other places.

Buried by succeeding deposits, and subjected to unbelievable heat and pressure, these basalts metamorphosed into "greenstones," so called because of the greenish cast imparted by heavy doses of epidote and chlorite. In some places, though, the rock is nearly purple in tone. The Catoctin greenstones are best appreciated in the northern and central parts of Shenandoah, lining the highest ridges and mountain summits. From Hemlock Springs Overlook to Swift Run Gap, Skyline Drive travels almost entirely through the Catoctin. In some locations, the formation is nearly 2,000 feet thick.

After the Catoctin was deposited, an ocean swept over the area, precipitating massive accumulations of sediments that were cemented into a suite of rock called the Chilhowee Group. This happened during the Cambrian Period, around 570 to 500 million years ago, a time known for an explosion of life forms. Early worms called *Skolithos* burrowed into the sediments that became these rocks, and left behind some of the earliest fossils found in Shenandoah.

It's time now for that big mountain-building episode mentioned earlier. Thousands of feet of buried rock, including those basement layers, were metamorphosed and raised perhaps as high as 15,000 to 20,000 feet in elevation. Today, Shenandoah's

tallest peak, Hawksbill, stands a mere 4,050 feet above the level of the sea. Thus, miles of mountains have been removed in the last 200 million years. Obviously, other forces came into play to shape the present landscape of Shenandoah. Those forces were weathering and erosion—the breakdown and removal of that material. Water and ice were the prime movers and shakers. Until about 10,000 years ago, North America was gripped in a series of cold spells. Though continental glaciers were not present in Shenandoah itself, they were close enough—only about 200 miles to the north—to render it at times a much chillier locale. The freezing and thawing of ice left fingerprints in the form of bare talus and scree slopes, as well as bedroom-sized boulders stranded in streambeds.

Though Shenandoah is definitely warmer

now, ice still freezes and thaws each year, expanding and contracting and wedging rocks out of place. But it is water, moving down steep hillsides, that now ushers the vast bulk of the mountains down to the sea, aided by the physical and chemical activities of plants and animals. Erosion, rather than uplift, holds the upper hand just now.

Geology determined how people moved and where they settled in these mountains. From the earliest arrivals, the favored crossings were at the gaps, or low points, where the bedrock was thinner or where a natural break, or fault, created a weak spot for wind or water to work a little faster. In the hollows and coves midway down the mountains, streams dropped fine sediment. There, farmers found the best soils for crops, and timbermen discovered the grandest hardwoods for their saws. Geology obviously dictated where miners dug for iron and copper too. Today, as a national park, Shenandoah's finest attributes ultimately are owed to geology: the grand views from Skyline Drive, the high peaks that hikers love to climb, the waterfalls that dance in the sunlight, and the soils that grow the green forests.

Geology is as much process as product. And the processes—the building up and the breaking down—occur in an endless cycle. Even in our brief lifetimes, we can see it everywhere we look—rocks fall, mud flows, streams churn. Yes, mountains do come and mountains do go. But while they're here, they do a good job of putting our lives in perspective.

ABOVE: The view from Stony Man Overlook. PHOTO ©MICHAEL COLLIER

WATERFALLS

Who can resist the beauty of a waterfall? Water, usually staying within the orderly confines of a stream or river, erupts in animation when it encounters a steep descent over rock. The sound, roaring or whispering, drowns out all others. Beside a waterfall, you can while away hours, cooled by the showery spray and spellbound by the progress of a single silvery strand of water.

Shenandoah National Park is blessed with waterfalls, and a trip to see one is always a delight. Getting to each falls, however, means walking; some are an easy mile or so, others mandate more than six miles roundtrip. All require going downhill first, followed by an often steep ascent coming back out.

For those into superlatives, the three tallest waterfalls in the park are Overall Run Falls (93 feet), Whiteoak Canyon Falls (86 feet), and South River Falls (83 feet). These steep cascades form when they meet the Catoctin greenstone, one of the primary rock formations in the park.

An easy one to reach is Dark Hollow Falls, a little less than a mile and a half roundtrip. The well-maintained trail follows Hogcamp Branch, the stream that drains out of Big Meadows Swamp and into the Rose River. The falls spill down 70 feet over four risers of rock, the sound of the water at first thready, then swelling in volume as it rejoins the main stream. Standing at the base of the falls, families click snapshots, then turn and go, taking their time trudging back up the steep trail.

South River Falls is a longer walk. The trail begins at the South River Picnic Area along Skyline Drive. In a little over a mile, the trail clings to the hillside while South River charges down into wilder terrain of thick woods and a tight gorge. The falls crash down the cliff, then split into two parts. Though the rugged canyon prohibits a close approach, hikers still get a stunning view of the falls from a rock-walled platform beside the trail.

The Shenandoah National Park Association's booklet *Hikes to Waterfalls* gives good detail on additional walks to Cedar Run, Rose River, Doyles River, Jones Run Falls and others.

OPPOSITE: The falls of Overall Run. PHOTO ©SCOTT T. SMITH   **ABOVE:** Whiteoak Falls, spring. PHOTO ©WILLARD CLAY

HUMAN HISTORY: TRACKS AND TRACES

These days, folks come to Shenandoah to revel in Nature in all her wondrous manifestations. But those who look more closely at the land discover the dim tracks and traces of people who've come before—moldering stone walls carpeted with spongy moss, a wizened apple tree, an old road overgrown with brambles.

Around 10,000 years ago, as the climate and the land became more welcoming, American Indians ascended the mountains. Seneca and Siouan relatives settled in the lowlands and journeyed here for food. They made camps, almost always near water, where they stopped long enough to chip out a stone knife or two before continuing the quest for bison, elk, berries, and nuts. In places like Big Meadows, where Indians started to make camps about 6,000 years ago, they may have set fires intentionally to encourage the bounty.

Until the late 1600s, American Indians continued to reap the region's resources. But the onslaught of warring groups from the north, and the arrival of Europeans, effectively ended their supremacy. New ideas of ownership and land use were imposed. With help from Indian guides, in March 1669 German settler John Lederer traveled from Jamestown into the mountains of Shenandoah, possibly at Swift Run Gap. From one point, he proclaimed, "To the North and West, my sight was suddenly bounded by Mountains higher than that I stood upon." Deep snow hampered Lederer's progress, until numbed by "the coldness of the Air and Earth together" he retreated the way he had come. Yet what John Lederer left was the first known written account of Shenandoah.

It would be a while before anyone came to stay. By the mid 1700s, the English were carving out expansive estates, such as the "manors" of Lord Fairfax, and Germans were obtaining patents to the best lands in the fertile Shenandoah Valley and within the future Shenandoah National Park. By the end of the 1700s, the valley's population was estimated at 67,000. The fine crops they raised needed to get to market, and thus came roads and

railroads.

Prosperity lasted for a time, but by 1860 sectionalism severed the country. The Confederates considered the Shenandoah Valley a "breadbasket" crucially important to their ultimate victory. Through the spring of 1862, General Thomas "Stonewall" Jackson and troops crossed the mountains and moved north down the valley, taking advantage of an all-weather turnpike. Though well outnumbered by Union troops, Jackson and his men won five battles during the 40-day campaign, using strategy considered brilliant by modern military planners. Other battles were fought in the val-

ley in 1864, with one at Overall Run very close to what would become Shenandoah National Park. Though the Confederates prevailed, only a short time later Union General Philip Sheridan swept through the valley and burned everything to the ground.

After the Civil War, several forces conspired in the early 20th century to hasten the decline of mountain farms, including the devastating chestnut blight and the change from barter to a cash economy.

At the turn of the new century, talk was circulating about a national park in the eastern United States. In 1924, talk turned to action when the U.S. Congress authorized the Southern Appalachian National Park Committee to study and recommend possible sites. At the same time, Shenandoah Valley boosters marshaled together to lobby for a park in the northern Blue Ridge Mountains. More than a thousand people attended a huge convention in January 1924; a direct outgrowth was formation of Shenandoah Valley, Incorporated, a strong advocate for creation of a national park. Not surprisingly, one of the biggest supporters was George Freeman Pollock, whose popular Skyland development was known to nearly everyone who came into the mountains. A noted Virginian, Harry Flood Byrd, Senior, governor of the state and later United States senator, owned a cabin at Skyland. He remained one of Shenandoah's staunchest, and most influential, friends.

All the lobbying efforts paid off. In 1926, the United States government simultaneously authorized Shenandoah and Great Smoky Mountains National

ABOVE: Artillery at New Market Historical Site, Shenandoah Valley. PHOTO ©MICHAEL J. HICKEY/PlacePhoto.com

Parks. But this was only the beginning. It would take another decade before the complex land purchases were made for Shenandoah. The state of Virginia had to raise money to pay for the lands that were condemned, a highly controversial action. Then the property was to be donated to the federal government for the park. Initial park boundary lines would have encompassed 521,000 acres, but it quickly became clear that the land would be far too expensive to buy. In 1928, the acreage was reduced to 321,000 acres, and halved again in 1932.

Some 450 families, perhaps 2,200 people, lived in what would become Shenandoah National Park. Among them were the Merchants, Dyers, Nicholsons, Corbins, Weakleys, Berrys, Taylors, and Shenks. Some residents were in favor of selling their land; others resisted. Declared one: "I do refuse to surrender possession of the land and buildings. . . .I do not feel like giving up my home and all that I possess for a sporting ground." Finally, in October 1934, those residents who refused to sell were given one month's notice to vacate their property.

Eventually more than a thousand separate parcels were obtained to create the national park. By spring 1938, according to park historian Reed Engle, "42 elderly residents had been given life estates, 175 families had been relocated to resettlement communities, several families had been physically evicted and their houses burned, and the majority of the mountain residents just left the mountain on their own." When Annie Shenk died in 1979, the last lifetime resident in the park had passed.

Even as the contentious purchases and reloca-

tions were taking place, work began on Skyline Drive. Civilian Conservation Corps camps were set up, charged with creating a "western national park experience" in the East. Finally, on July 3, 1936, Shenandoah National Park was dedicated, before a crowd of thousands seated on chestnut logs in Big Meadows. To a nation tuned in on the radio, President Franklin D. Roosevelt orated: "This park is in the largest sense a work of conser-

vation. . . .we are preserving the beauty and the wealth of the hills, and the mountains and the plains and the trees and the streams. . . .we are enriching the character and happiness of our people."

Then, it was time to ready the new park for visitors. Though George Freeman Pollock worked tirelessly to be selected to provide those services, he lost out in 1937 to the Virginia Sky-Line Company. This group of Richmond business people won the government contract to develop lodges, campgrounds, and other facilities in Shenandoah. Dickey Ridge, Big Meadows, and Elkwallow were

the first to be built. As a reflection of the "separate but equal" doctrine of the time, Lewis Mountain campground and picnic area opened in 1940 "for Negroes only." Though it began as a segregated area, after World War II Shenandoah National Park was one of the first places in Virginia to be integrated.

Many original buildings were torn down as part of park development (or they deteriorated during the war, when visitation dwindled and work largely ceased). But the years have rendered history a more valued part of the Shenandoah story, and a number of properties have been placed on the National Register of Historic Places. In one effort, the Park Service has restored and reopened an historic landmark to visitors: Rapidan Camp, or Camp Hoover, on the headwaters of the Rapidan River. From 1929 to 1932, this was the "summer White House" of President Herbert Hoover and his wife Lou. Three cabins, walkways, pools, and plantings have been brought back to their 1931 appearance, when the President came up on weekends to enjoy the cool shade of this refuge and conduct some of the nation's business. When Hoover wasn't working, he fished for rainbow trout, while his wife naturalized wild orchids in informal gardens and furnished the canvas tent cabins. And though they were "at the end of nowhere," as Mrs. Hoover saw it, they still had electricity, a telephone, and mail dropped from an airplane.

With nearly 40 percent of Shenandoah officially designated wilderness, nature does prevail here. But still, the tracks and traces on the land won't be forgotten.

ABOVE: Prime Minister's Cabin at Hoover Camp. PHOTO ©PAT & CHUCK BLACKLEY
PAGE 20/21: Sunset seen from Thorofare Mountain. PHOTO ©SCOTT T. SMITH

SKYLAND RESORT & MASSANUTTEN LODGE

No story of Shenandoah is complete without mention of Skyland and George Freeman Pollock. Steadfast park booster and inveterate showman, Pollock took over his father's interests in Stony Man Camp in the late 1880s, sold lots in the area, and developed lodging and dining at what became the ever-popular Skyland resort.

Early on, people from Washington, D.C. took the train to Luray, spent the night there, then came up to Skyland by carriage road to partake in an array of activities. As they opened their eyes each morning to Pollock's bugle call, guests could choose from a packed schedule of hikes, horseback rides, campouts, masquerade balls, jousting matches, parties, and pow wows.

George Freeman Pollock was so busy trying to make ends meet at Skyland that he had not taken time to marry. All that changed in 1911, when at age 43 he married Addie Nairn Hunter. Divorced and well set with her own money, Addie succumbed to George's charms and married him. She had purchased a lot at Skyland and hired architect Victor Mindeleff to design a cabin. This was Massanutten Lodge, and it became George and Addie's home for a time.

The cabin's architecture was classic Arts and Crafts style. The exterior was covered with interesting rough-bark chestnut siding, and the chimney was native stone. The porch faced west for an inspiring view. The living room was furnished with wicker chairs, a big fireplace, and shelves filled with popular books of the day such as Gene Stratton Porter's *Girl of the Limberlost*. An avid gardener, Addie tended lilacs and peonies in terraced gardens surrounding the home. By all accounts, she much preferred playing her piano or enjoying a quiet card game with her neighbors, the Judds, Fells, and Senator Harry Byrd Senior. Addie's marriage to George hit rocky times, and by 1920 they no longer shared her cabin.

In 1936, the Park Service awarded Addie lifetime tenancy at Massanutten Lodge. By then, poor health prevented her from spending time there. She died in 1944 in Washington, D.C. George Pollock died in 1949, and his ashes were scattered over Skyland.

In 2001 the Park Service restored Massanutten Lodge, replacing the chestnut bark siding and faithfully refurnishing the interior based on old photographs. Park rangers escort visitors inside, where they can sit in the gracious living room and imagine life in the Pollocks' day.

ABOVE: Cottage at Skyland. PHOTO ©PAT & CHUCK BLACKLEY

OPPOSITE: Ferns at Stony Man. PHOTO ©MICHAEL COLLIER

VISITING THE PARK

On a May afternoon with a storm threatening, I join a group of visitors going out for a walk into Big Meadows with Ranger John. Right off the bat, he announces that he's a coward and will beat a hasty retreat should lightning be in evidence. We dutifully nod in agreement when he adds a footnote about two fellow rangers who've been struck but lived to tell about it.

We follow John out into the big grassy bowl, amid golden ragwort, bluets, and blueberry bushes. Once, Big Meadows was more than a thousand acres of prime pastureland. The Lamb family owned a large portion, but it was the Weakleys, tenant farmers, who tended the cows brought up to graze from spring to fall.

John leads us over to see the foundations of the Weakley cabin at the far edge of the meadow. With 12 children, Emma Weakley had plenty of help herding the animals. She was known for her cooking, and she grew a big garden and canned and preserved much of their food. We pass around an old photo of Emma on her porch, a gorgeous crazy quilt draped over the railing.

But in 1933, in her eighth decade, Emma Weakley's self-sufficient life changed drastically. Nearly 200 young men descended practically in her front yard to take up residence at the newly erected Civilian Conservation Corps camp. Their mission was to help build Shenandoah National Park.

Today, Emma Weakley might not recognize Big Meadows. Hawthorns, black locust, pin cherries, and various other trees and shrubs have invaded, shrinking the grassland to a mere 130 acres. To keep part of the meadow open, the Park Service has instituted a cycle of mowing, burning, and letting the ground lay fallow. Deer love the edge between meadow and forest, and have sheared a sharp browse line in the gray dogwoods. Foxes are seen, John reports, and the howls of coyotes sometimes fill the meadow. Along with the wild things, John relishes his work in Shenandoah because he has the opportunity to see families coming back again and again, even watching the kids grow up.

Located midway along Skyline Drive, Big Meadows is one of the most popular places to visit in Shenandoah National Park. At 3,500 feet, it's cool most of the year, and the large campground, lodge, and nearby hiking trails draw many people. The main Harry Byrd, Senior, Visitor Center is also located at Big Meadows, with exhibits and films, a well-stocked book and map sales area, and a schedule of seasonal ranger talks and programs, which are also listed in the park visitor guide, *Shenandoah Overlook*. Loft Mountain Information Center is 30 miles south of Big Meadows, Dickey Ridge Visitor Center is about 45 miles to the north. The Dickey Ridge Visitor Center occupies a 1930s rock and stone building that once served as a dining hall. If you come in

TOP
Skyline Drive, autumn.
PHOTO ©JEFF GNASS
MIDDLE
White-tailed deer in Big Meadows.
PHOTO ©MICHAEL J. HICKEY/PlacePhoto.com
BOTTOM
Snag near Skyland.
PHOTO ©LAURENCE PARENT

OPPOSITE: Trail across Big Meadows. PHOTO ©JERRY L. WHALEY

TOP
The view from Jewell Ridge.
PHOTO ©PAT & CHUCK BLACKLEY
MIDDLE
Male northern cardinal.
PHOTO ©ADAM JONES
BOTTOM
Winter along the Hughes River.
PHOTO ©CHARLES GURCHE

the park's north entrance, this is a good first stop, with an orientation film and lifelike exhibits of Shenandoah's natural treasures—turkey-tail fungus, raccoons, groundhogs, copperheads, eastern screech owls in old apple trees, and monarch butterflies on milkweed.

Along Skyline Drive, it's advisable to go into "mosey" gear, slowing down to take in the scenery and stopping often for the panoramic views. Pick out major landmarks, linger for a picnic, stretch your legs on a hike, watch for wildlife, and savor a sunset.

Park campgrounds are located at Mathews Arm (mile 22.2), Big Meadows (mile 51), Lewis Mountain (mile 57.5), and Loft Mountain (mile 79.5). Dundo Camp (mile 83.7) is for groups. Backcountry camping is also possible with a free park permit; camps must be set up 30 feet from any stream. In the backcountry, and throughout the park, visitors are urged to practice leave-no-trace stewardship: plan ahead, travel and camp on durable surfaces, dispose of waste properly, leave what you find, minimize campfire impacts, respect wildlife, and be considerate of other visitors.

Showers and laundry services are available at Big Meadows, Lewis Mountain, and Loft Mountain. For a little more "civilization," lodging is available at Skyland (mile 41-42), Big Meadows, and Lewis Mountain. For more rustic accommodations, the Potomac Appalachian Trail Club maintains six hike-in cabins in the park.

Full meals and grill food can be ordered at Skyland, Big Meadows, Elkwallow, and Loft Mountain. Gasoline is available in the park at Elkwallow, Big Meadows, and Loft Mountain waysides, along with groceries, some camping supplies, and souvenirs.

For a more in-depth experience, the park offers a selection of field seminars. For information, contact the Park Education Office (540) 999-3489, or visit the Web site: www.nps.gov/shen/seminars.

Shenandoah's extensive trail system allows hikes of nearly any length and degree of difficulty. Park trails are well marked with concrete posts and blue blazes. Aluminum bands on the posts give trail names and directions. The Appalachian Trail is marked with white blazes, while yellow blazes indicate trails open to horseback riders. If you don't have your own horse, you can contact Skyland Stables for guided rides. Bicyclists must stay to paved areas. It's possible to pedal Skyline Drive, but blind curves and narrow road shoulders present real challenges.

For anglers, Shenandoah's many miles of high-mountain streams are irresistible. Fishing is allowed with a valid state license, and regulations and information on stream openings can be obtained at visitor centers. Most is catch-and-release, but a few streams are open to harvest.

Shenandoah and Skyline Drive are open year-round. Visitor centers and concessioner facilities generally are open from April or May through October and November.

SHENANDOAH NATIONAL PARK

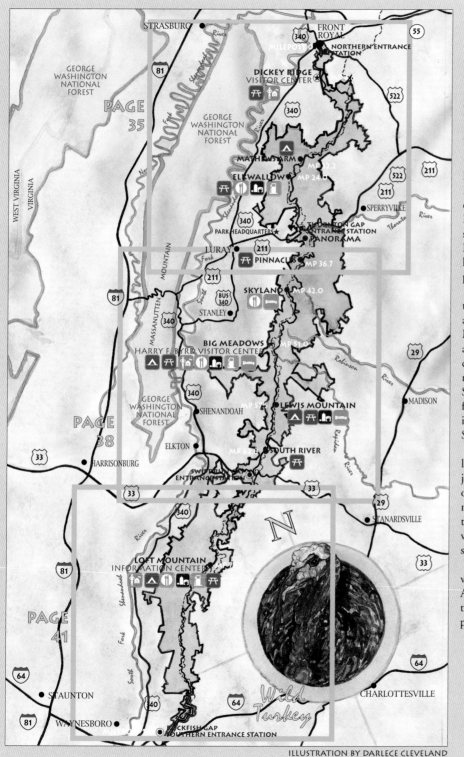

Shenandoah National Park encompasses more than 197,000 acres in the mountains of west-central Virginia. The park's strikingly irregular boundary reveals its creation from many private parcels of land in the 1930s. In places, the park narrows down to only a mile in width.

Skyline Drive, the main thoroughfare, allows access to the park's front- and backcountry. For the most part, the drive follows the summit of the Blue Ridge for 105 miles north to south. From the doorstep at the town of Front Royal, southbound travelers gain elevation in a hurry. In only three miles, Shenandoah Valley Overlook, at nearly 1,400 feet, gives a glimpse of the park's namesake valley to the west.

The mountains continue to rise, with more than 60 peaks in the park exceeding 3,000 feet above sea level. Two—Hawksbill Peak and Stony Man—top out at more than 4,000 feet. Largely a barrier to early travel, the mountain front was crossed at the low points, or gaps. The main roads into the park still do so—at Thornton, Swift Run, and Rockfish Gaps. Clear, spring-fed streams tumble down the hillsides, draining into the watersheds of three major rivers—the Shenandoah, Rappahannock, and James.

The Appalachian Trail closely parallels Skyline Drive in the park. Hikers can join and rejoin the "AT" at numerous road crossings and overlooks. Along with the 100-plus miles of this national trail, the park's own internal trail system includes about 400 additional miles, providing walking opportunities from short nature strolls to backcountry trips of many days.

Nearly all the park land is forest now, providing sanctuary for plants, animals, and people. As President Franklin Roosevelt proclaimed at the park's dedication, Shenandoah would be a place both of recreation and re-creation.

ILLUSTRATION BY DARLECE CLEVELAND

PAGE 28/29: Foggy sunrise view of the Piedmont seen from Old Rag Mountain. PHOTO ©CHARLES GURCHE

MOUNTAIN ENTERPRISES

"There was lots of activity during picking time. It probably took about everybody in Harmony Hollow to get the work done. Workers would also come up from Browntown Valley. There was so much weight from boxes of apples on the wagons. . .that the brakes would have to be used on the back wheels all the time when coming down the very steep orchard roads."

Hoping the brakes would hold the wheels was an everyday challenge for farmers in these steep-sided mountains. In the century before Shenandoah became a national park, some people made trips back and forth from what they called "home farms" in the valleys up to their mountain farms. Contrary to the convenient stereotype of the poor, illiterate mountaineer living in isolation up in some dark "holler," these rural Virginians engaged in many enterprises and maintained a lively network of trade. The park is threaded with former routes of commerce that have reverted to footpaths. There were churches, schools, stores, mills, and post offices, and tourists introduced city-bred ways.

Residents sold or bartered produce from their gardens and orchards—cabbages, corn, beans, and fruit. With a team and two-horse wagon, they'd get a load of the popular Milam apples, a variety that was developed around Milam Gap. In summer, people drove their cattle up to the high meadows to graze on the good grass. The magnificent old hardwood trees were taken out for lumber, and the bark was sold to tanneries. Some bought land or mineral rights for the copper it contained, while others harnessed stream power to run gristmills and distilleries. They split chestnut fence rails and made hickory barrel hoops. Work was nonstop Monday through Saturday but Sunday was the Lord's Day. Most people would not even go fishing on the Sabbath.

Most priceless were the delicious chestnuts. Said one early resident, "We'd go and get a sack of chestnuts in the morning then after dinner walk down to the store and sell them and get a bag of groceries." But with the devastating arrival of the chestnut blight, by the 1920s nearly all the American chestnut trees were gone. By that time, many Shenandoah residents had joined in the cash economy of early 20th-century America, buying toys and tools and shoes, even cars.

ABOVE: Apples for sale in a roadside market. PHOTO ©PAT & CHUCK BLACKLEY

OPPOSITE: Yellow poplar forest in fog. PHOTO ©CHARLES GURCHE

TOURING
SKYLINE DRIVE

For many visitors, the two-lane blacktop Skyline Drive *is* Shenandoah National Park. The road stays to the narrow rooftop of the park, from Mile 0 at Front Royal, Virginia, to Mile 105 at Rockfish Gap. Along the way, nearly 70 overlooks permit expansive observations east to the Piedmont and west to the Shenandoah Valley and Massanutten Mountain. Years ago, landscape architect Harvey Benson stated, "It is for these far-reaching views from the Skyline Drive that the park is most widely known."

The idea of a scenic drive following the crest of the mountains was conceived just as the automobile was coming into its own in the United States. One of the earliest proposals for such a road came in 1924 from the group backing creation of Shenandoah National Park. Virginia's Senator Harry Byrd, Senior, proclaimed that it would be "the wonder way" by which people would travel in their own vehicles to see the new national park.

As land was still being acquired for the park, construction on the Skyline Drive began. On July 18, 1931, ground was broken at Skyland resort. The Central District section was the first to open to traffic in 1934. The North District opened in 1936, and the drive was completed in the South District in 1939. Contract laborers built the actual roadbed, while men with the Civilian Conservation Corps and other Depression-era employment programs constructed walls and overlooks, landscaped, and performed many other tasks. All were considered decent-paying jobs during the extreme economic times of the Thirties.

Skyline Drive has changed little today. Simple concrete mile markers, numbered north to south, point the way. Top speed is 35 miles an hour. At Skyland the road achieves its highest elevation—3,680 feet above sea level. Overlooks, picnic areas, campgrounds, and trails, including the Appalachian Trail, give visitors plenty of opportunity to stop and savor the grand views of the mountains, valleys, forests, and streams, and all the small things in between. White-tailed deer, wild turkey, and groundhogs frequent the road edges, and drivers are advised to watch for them. It's always a pleasure to observe these creatures in their native home.

TOP
Morning at Hazel Mountain Overlook. PHOTO ©JEFF GNASS
ABOVE
White-tailed deer. PHOTO ©ADAM JONES

OPPOSITE: The sinuous path of Skyline Drive. PHOTO ©CHARLES GURCHE

TOP
Jewell Hollow Overlook.
PHOTO ©PAT & CHUCK BLACKLEY
MIDDLE
Winter sunrise at Thornton Gap.
PHOTO ©CHARLES GURCHE
BOTTOM
Overall Run Falls.
PHOTO ©SCOTT T. SMITH

MILE O-31 (NORTH DISTRICT)

At the edge of the busy town of Front Royal, travelers immediately enter the park. Elevation here is 590 feet, lowest on Skyline Drive. In the 5 miles to Dickey Ridge Visitor Center, you climb to 1,900 feet.

5.0. Dickey Ridge Visitor Center is a worthwhile stop, for the orientation film, exhibits, publications, and on-duty rangers. The Dickey Ridge and Fox Hollow trails are accessible across the road. (In local parlance, a hollow is a valley between ridges.) Along the pleasant 1.2-mile loop through Fox Hollow, you'll see an old cemetery, rock walls, cherry trees, and other traces of the Fox family's pre-park homesite.

5.7. From **Signal Knob**, messages were relayed for the Confederates during the Civil War. In 1862, "Stonewall" Jackson moved his troops across the mountains down into the Shenandoah Valley. Said Jackson, "If the valley is lost, Virginia is lost." In November, Stonewall and his Confederates returned over the mountains. Jackson was wounded at Chancellorsville in 1863, and died a few days later. He is buried in Lexington, Virginia.

7.3. Gooney Manor Overlook. Gooney Manor in Browntown Valley was one of the large inherited land holdings of Thomas, the sixth Lord Fairfax, in the mid 1700s. Gooney was the name of his dog. One of Lord Fairfax's land surveyors was a teenager named George Washington.

10.4. At **Compton Gap**, the Appalachian Trail first crosses Skyline Drive, and the Blue Ridge proper begins.

10.8. From the gap the road ascends again, up to 2,400 feet at **Indian Run Overlook**. Here is a fine view east into Virginia's Piedmont, literally the "foot of the mountains," and a closer look at the prevalent rock, called a greenstone.

13.8. Hogwallow Flats, at an elevation of 2,665 feet, offers another big view of the Piedmont and the town of Flint Hill, where some families moved when their land was purchased for Shenandoah National Park.

17.1. Range View, just over 2,800 feet, is one of the best in this section on a clear day. You can look toward the Piedmont, and southwest down the length of the Blue Ridge at some of the highest peaks in the park: Hazel Mountain, Old Rag, The Pinnacle, Marys Rock, Stony Man, and Pass Mountain.

19.0. Mount Marshall Overlook. Mount Marshall dominates this section. It was named for Supreme Court Chief Justice John Marshall, who obtained one of Lord Fairfax's huge "manors" in the 1800s, which included parts of North and South Marshall Peaks.

20.8. At **Hogback Overlook** elevation exceeds 3,000 feet. Watch for turkey vultures soaring in the sky, and white-tailed deer grazing beside road. The trail to Overall Run Falls begins here; at 93 feet, it's the park's highest waterfall. It's a 6.5-mile roundtrip walk to see it.

22.2. Mathews Arm Campground is open May through October. Black bear sightings reputedly a good possibility here.

24.0. Elkwallow Wayside. Food, ice, gasoline, and campstore located here May-October. At the picnic area, you'll find the trailhead for Jeremys Run, a lovely mountain stream whose sycamore-shaded pools harbor trout.

31.5. Thornton Gap was named for Francis Thornton, who built Montpelier Mansion nearby in the Piedmont. His daughter, Mary, is the person for whom Marys Rock allegedly is named. US Highway 211 crosses here, heading east to Washington, D.C. and west to park headquarters, the town of Luray and Luray Caverns, and Interstate 81. This has been a cross-mountain road for a long time. As early as the mid 1700s, an inn at the gap provided overnight lodging for stagecoach and wagon passengers. The small Panorama development is a park visitor center.

MILE 31-65 (CENTRAL DISTRICT)

32.2. Marys Rock Tunnel is the only tunnel on Skyline Drive. It was finished in January 1932, and bored through more than 600 feet of the oldest rock visible along the drive—dating to a billion years!

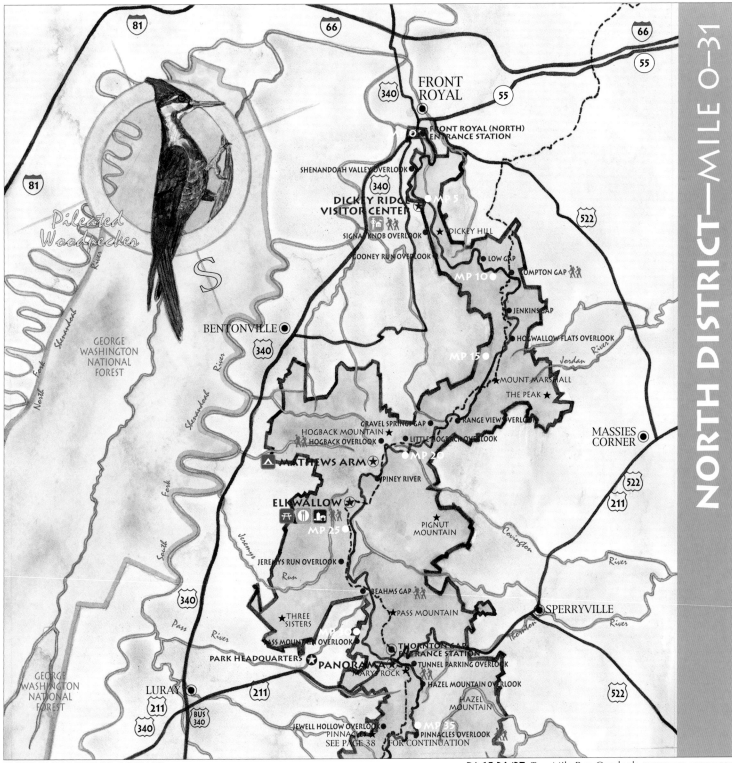

81

66

66

55

FRONT ROYAL

340

55

340

FRONT ROYAL (NORTH) ENTRANCE STATION

SHENANDOAH VALLEY OVERLOOK

340

522

DICKEY RIDGE VISITOR CENTER

MP 5

DICKEY HILL

SIGNAL KNOB OVERLOOK

GOONEY RUN OVERLOOK

LOW GAP

COMPTON GAP

MP 10

81

Pileated Woodpecker

S

JENKINS GAP

HOGWALLOW FLATS OVERLOOK

Jordan River

BENTONVILLE

340

GEORGE WASHINGTON NATIONAL FOREST

MP 15

MOUNT MARSHALL

THE PEAK

Shenandoah River

North Fork Shenandoah River

South Fork Shenandoah River

GRAVEL SPRINGS GAP

RANGE VIEW OVERLOOK

MASSIES CORNER

HOGBACK MOUNTAIN

HOGBACK OVERLOOK

LITTLE HOGBACK OVERLOOK

MP 20

MATTHEWS ARM

PINEY RIVER

522

211

ELKWALLOW

MP 25

PIGNUT MOUNTAIN

Covington River

JEREMYS RUN OVERLOOK

Jeremys Run

340

BEAHMS GAP

THREE SISTERS

PASS MOUNTAIN

SPERRYVILLE

Thornton River

Pass River

MP 30

PASS MOUNTAIN OVERLOOK

THORNTON GAP ENTRANCE STATION

PARK HEADQUARTERS

PANORAMA

MARYS ROCK

TUNNEL PARKING OVERLOOK

HAZEL MOUNTAIN OVERLOOK

LURAY

211

211

HAZEL MOUNTAIN

522

GEORGE WASHINGTON NATIONAL FOREST

211

BUS 340

340

JEWELL HOLLOW OVERLOOK

PINNACLES

SEE PAGE 38 FOR CONTINUATION

MP 35

PINNACLES OVERLOOK

ILLUSTRATION BY DARLECE CLEVELAND

PAGE 36/37: Two Mile Run Overlook. PHOTO ©TIM FITZHARRIS

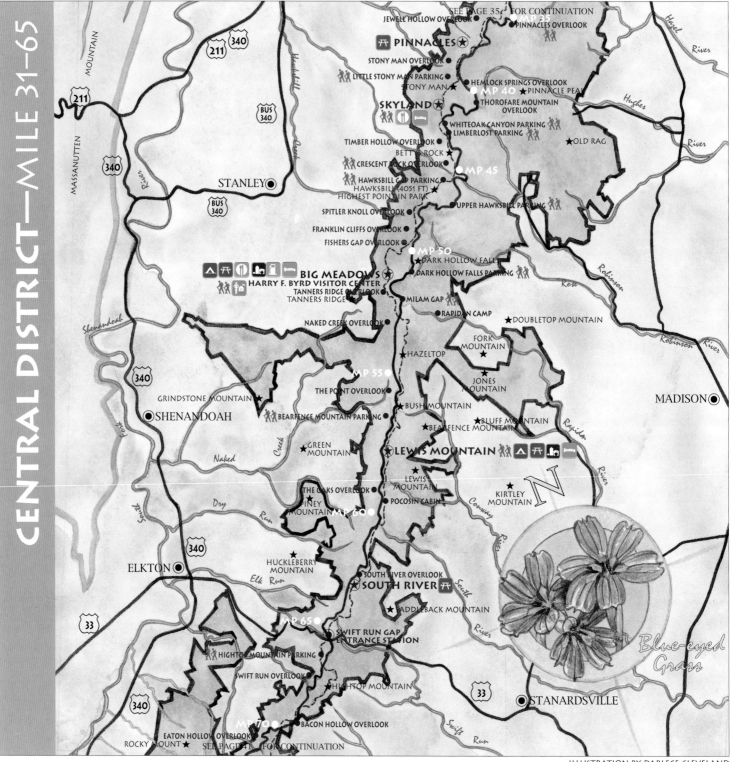

MASSANUTTEN MOUNTAIN

211
340
211
340

BUS 340

STANLEY

BUS 340

Shenandoah River

SHENANDOAH

340

SEE PAGE 35 FOR CONTINUATION
JEWELL HOLLOW OVERLOOK
PINNACLES OVERLOOK
MP 35
PINNACLES
STONY MAN OVERLOOK
LITTLE STONY MAN PARKING
HEMLOCK SPRINGS OVERLOOK
STONY MAN
MP 40
PINNACLE PEAK
SKYLAND
THOROFARE MOUNTAIN OVERLOOK
WHITEOAK CANYON PARKING
LIMBERLOST PARKING
OLD RAG
TIMBER HOLLOW OVERLOOK
BETTYS ROCK
CRESCENT ROCK OVERLOOK
MP 45
HAWKSBILL GAP PARKING
HAWKSBILL (4051 FT)
HIGHEST POINT IN PARK
UPPER HAWKSBILL PARKING
SPITLER KNOLL OVERLOOK
FRANKLIN CLIFFS OVERLOOK
FISHERS GAP OVERLOOK
MP 50
DARK HOLLOW FALLS
BIG MEADOWS
DARK HOLLOW FALLS PARKING
HARRY F. BYRD VISITOR CENTER
MILAM GAP
TANNERS RIDGE OVERLOOK
TANNERS RIDGE
RAPIDAN CAMP
DOUBLETOP MOUNTAIN
NAKED CREEK OVERLOOK
FORK MOUNTAIN
HAZELTOP
MP 55
THE POINT OVERLOOK
JONES MOUNTAIN
GRINDSTONE MOUNTAIN
BUSH MOUNTAIN
BLUFF MOUNTAIN
BEARFENCE MOUNTAIN PARKING
BEARFENCE MOUNTAIN
GREEN MOUNTAIN
LEWIS MOUNTAIN
THE OAKS OVERLOOK
LEWIS MOUNTAIN
PINEY MOUNTAIN
POCOSIN CABIN
KIRTLEY MOUNTAIN
MP 60
HUCKLEBERRY MOUNTAIN
SOUTH RIVER OVERLOOK
ELKTON
Elk Run
SOUTH RIVER
SADDLEBACK MOUNTAIN
MP 65
SWIFT RUN GAP ENTRANCE STATION
33
HIGHTOP MOUNTAIN PARKING
SWIFT RUN OVERLOOK
HIGHTOP MOUNTAIN
33
STANARDSVILLE
340
MP 70
BACON HOLLOW OVERLOOK
EATON HOLLOW OVERLOOK
ROCKY MOUNT
SEE PAGE 41 FOR CONTINUATION

MADISON

N

Blue-eyed Grass

Hawksbill Creek
Naked Creek
Dry Run
Piney River
South Fork Shenandoah River
Rose River
Robinson River
Hughes River
Hazel River
Rapidan River
Conway River
Swift Run

ILLUSTRATION BY DARLECE CLEVELAND

33.5. Meadow Spring Parking Area. The trail to Marys Rock begins here (2.8 miles roundtrip), and includes a lovely stretch of the Appalachian Trail. Once at the top, you look down 1,200 feet on Thornton Gap and have wonderful views west and east.

41.7–42.5. Skyland. Here, you've reached the highest point on Skyline Drive—3,680 feet above sea level. Skyland was originally George Freeman Pollock's Stony Man Camp. From 1906 until 1936 he operated it as Skyland resort. Today, it is a modern lodge, with restaurant, gift shop, and cabins.

Pollock guided guests to the top of Stony Man Mountain, along the same trail visitors take today (1.6 miles). On a walk to the summit in 1886, he exclaimed: "Climb, climb, and climb, up and up as though we were going into the sky. Was I thrilled! We proceeded onto the peak and what a view. To say that I was carried away is putting it mildly. I raved and shouted." People today often share that sentiment when they get to the top.

42.6. Whiteoak Canyon. Whiteoak is a beautiful mountain stream lined with big trees; a popular hike of just over 4 miles roundtrip leads to upper Whiteoak Canyon Falls. Down the road at mile 43 is the Limberlost Trail, a wheelchair-accessible path with benches along the way. Formerly lined with grand old eastern hemlocks, the trees were killed by an invading insect, the hemlock wooly adelgid, and have been cut down. But the mountain laurel blooming in June is still breathtaking.

46.7. Upper Hawksbill Parking Area. This moderate uphill trail leads a mile to Hawksbill Mountain, the highest peak in Shenandoah. From the observation platform at 4,050 feet above sea level, among fir and spruce, the view to the west and north is stupendous. Keen eyes may spot a peregrine falcon slashing across the sky. More likely, you'll be entertained by vultures tilting in the wind, enjoying the same view. The stone Byrds Nest Shelter No. 2 at the top is a day-use shelter for hikers.

51–51.2. Big Meadows has been another center of visitor activity in the park for many years. Located here are Byrd Visitor Center, Big Meadows Lodge, coffee shop, campstore, gas station, campground, picnic area, and trailheads.

Recent evidence points to American Indian presence in Big Meadows by about 6,000 years ago. By the mid 1850s Anglo settlers had arrived and were farming and grazing their livestock. A CCC camp was set up in the meadow in 1933, and it is here that President Franklin D. Roosevelt dedicated Shenandoah National Park in 1936. With park establishment, grazing and farming were no longer allowed.

Because black locusts and other shrubs and trees were encroaching, the Park Service maintains part of Big Meadows to keep it grassy and open. There is also a swampy area that intrigues historians and biologists, who are trying to learn why it exists. The swamp harbors the rare smooth green snake and several unusual plants.

51.3. Rapidan Road goes to Rapidan Camp. Also known as Camp Hoover, this was the "Summer White House" for President Herbert Hoover and Lou Henry Hoover. It has been restored to its 1931 appearance.

52.8. From **Milam Gap**, the Mill Prong Trail leads to Rapidan Camp. Check at Byrd Visitor Center for van tours at certain times of year as well.

57.5. Lewis Mountain Campground. This small, quiet campground also has a picnic ground, campstore, shower, and a few cabins for rent.

59.5. Pocosin Cabin. The cabin, built in 1936 by the CCC, is one of six backcountry cabins that can be rented through the Potomac Appalachian Trail Club.

62.8. South River Picnic Area. A large, shaded picnic area and beginning of the trail to South River Falls.

65.5. Swift Run Gap. US Highway 33 crosses at this gap, heading west to the towns of Elkton and Harrisonburg. Like Thornton Gap, this has been another significant crossing of the Blue Ridge Mountains for a long time. German scholar

TOP
Rocks atop Hawksbill Mountain.
PHOTO ©MICHAEL COLLIER
ABOVE
Autumn in Whiteoak Canyon.
PHOTO ©CHARLES GURCHE

TOP
Dense fog along the Appalachian Trail near Skyland. PHOTO ©TERRY DONNELLY
MIDDLE
Jones Run Falls.
PHOTO ©CHARLES GURCHE

John Lederer possibly first saw the Blue Ridge here in 1669, and Governor Alexander Spotswood and his expedition may also have passed through in September 1716 on their way to the Shenandoah Valley. (Some historians think Milam Gap was more likely.) A plaque at the gap commemorates this event.

MILE 65-105 (SOUTH DISTRICT)

From Swift Run Gap, Skyline Drive passes through the park's South District, the quieter end of Shenandoah.

66.7. Just south of the gap, you arrive at the trailhead for **Hightop**. It's 1.2 miles one-way along the Appalachian Trail to the top of the highest peak in the South District—3,587 feet above sea level. Enjoy the exuberant trillium blooms in spring, a perfectly good excuse to pause and catch your breath during the 900-foot ascent.

69.3. Bacon Hollow Overlook sits very near the park's eastern boundary. The view stares 1,500 feet down into Bacon Hollow, a small Piedmont town. Check out the billion-year-old Pedlar granites here—last chance to see them if you're heading south.

73.2. Simmons Gap. Ranger station located here, with a fire road that follows an old trace through the mountains.

76.2. Two Mile Run Overlook. Look north to Two Mile Ridge and west to the abrupt southern tip of Massanutten Mountain, which has dominated the scene for the greater part of the Skyline Drive. A demanding trail to Rocky Mount begins here.

77.5. Ivy Creek. The Appalachian Trail crosses through this overlook. A short walk shows fine rock construction, along with a dramatic drop into rugged terrain to the east. You'll enjoy immediate peacefulness as you leave the road behind. The sign here informs hikers that it's 2 million steps ahead to Springer Mountain, Georgia, and 3 million steps back to Mount Katahdin in Maine: perhaps encouragement to southbound through-hikers on the AT that they're more than halfway there!

79.5. Loft Mountain. Located here is the last campground on the drive for southbound travelers. The Frazier Discovery Trail is a pleasant 1.3-mile loop up to the top of Loft Mountain. It passes through former pasture and fields being filled in with young saplings. The wayside has a gas station, campstore, and restaurant. The park information station is open spring to fall.

81.1. Doyles River Parking Area. Access for the Doyles River Trail and Upper and Lower Doyles River Falls, a 3.2-mile-roundtrip if you go all the way to the lower falls.

81.2. Big Run Overlook. Several good circuit hikes start here for exploration of the park's wilderness and largest watershed.

83.7. Dundo Campground. A former CCC camp, Dundo is now the park's group campground.

84.1. Jones Run. Hike to lovely Jones Run Falls, 3.4 miles roundtrip.

84.8. Blackrock. It's a fairly easy mile roundtrip to the top of Blackrock, a pile of bare quartzite with a spectacular view. Through much of the 19th and into the 20th centuries, people went to Blackrock Springs Resort to partake of the healing waters.

90.0. Riprap Parking Area. Trail to Chimney Rock, a steep hike of 3.4 miles roundtrip through wilderness to a big wall of whitish quartzite.

94.2. Turk Gap. A gradual hike to the top of Turk Mountain (2.2 miles roundtrip), into "official" park wilderness. Check the rock for fossils of 500-million-year-old worm burrows.

98.9. Calf Mountain Overlook. An expansive vista from one end of the overlook to the other, offering final views of the Shenandoah Valley, with the city of Waynesboro down in the valley to the west.

105.4. Rockfish Gap. This is the southern terminus of the Skyline Drive, at an elevation of 1,900 feet. The Blue Ridge Parkway joins here, a fascinating and scenic road that continues another 469 miles through the southern Appalachians to Great Smoky Mountains National Park. US 250 and Interstate 64 cross at Rockfish Gap, west to Waynesboro and east to Charlottesville. Hawk watchers station themselves here in the fall to count migrating raptors.

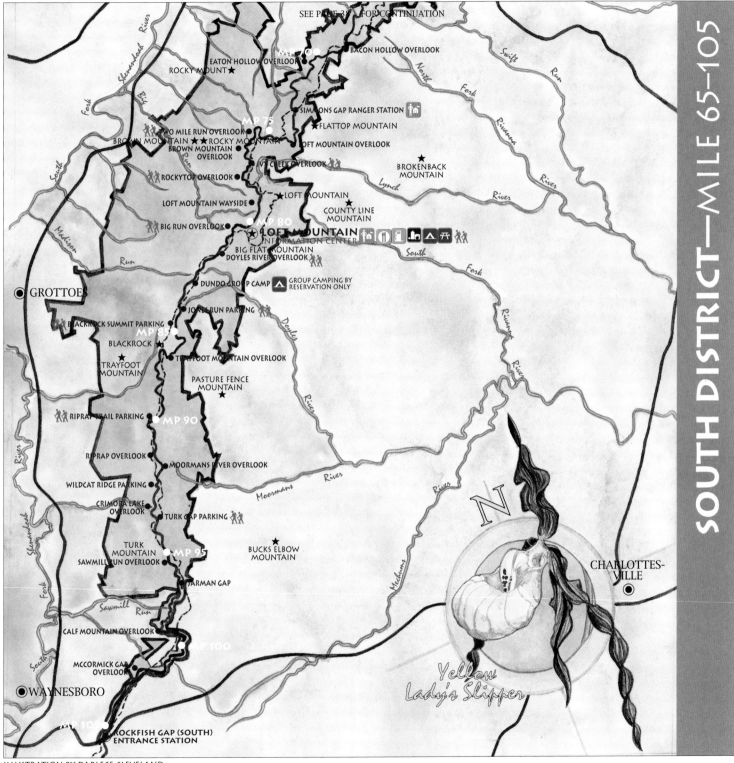

SEE PAGE 31 FOR CONTINUATION

BACON HOLLOW OVERLOOK

MP 70

EATON HOLLOW OVERLOOK
ROCKY MOUNT ★

SIMMONS GAP RANGER STATION

MP 75
★ FLATTOP MOUNTAIN

TWO MILE RUN OVERLOOK
BROWN MOUNTAIN ★★ ROCKY MOUNTAIN
BROWN MOUNTAIN
OVERLOOK
IVY CREEK OVERLOOK

LOFT MOUNTAIN OVERLOOK

BROKENBACK
MOUNTAIN ★

ROCKYTOP OVERLOOK

LOFT MOUNTAIN WAYSIDE
★ LOFT MOUNTAIN

COUNTY LINE
MOUNTAIN ★

BIG RUN OVERLOOK
MP 80
LOFT MOUNTAIN
INFORMATION CENTER

BIG FLAT MOUNTAIN
DOYLES RIVER OVERLOOK

DUNDO GROUP CAMP
GROUP CAMPING BY
RESERVATION ONLY

GROTTOES

JONES RUN PARKING

BLACKROCK SUMMIT PARKING
MP 85
BLACKROCK ★

TRAYFOOT MOUNTAIN OVERLOOK

TRAYFOOT
MOUNTAIN ★

PASTURE FENCE
MOUNTAIN ★

RIPRAP TRAIL PARKING
MP 90

RIPRAP OVERLOOK
MOORMANS RIVER OVERLOOK

WILDCAT RIDGE PARKING

CRIMORA LAKE
OVERLOOK
TURK GAP PARKING

TURK
MOUNTAIN ★
MP 95
BUCKS ELBOW
MOUNTAIN ★

SAWMILL RUN OVERLOOK

JARMAN GAP

CALF MOUNTAIN OVERLOOK

MP 100

MCCORMICK GAP
OVERLOOK

WAYNESBORO

CHARLOTTES-
VILLE

N

Yellow
Lady's Slipper

MP 105
ROCKFISH GAP (SOUTH)
ENTRANCE STATION

ILLUSTRATION BY DARLECE CLEVELAND

THE CIVILIAN CONSERVATION CORPS

Within a month of delivering his inaugural speech, President Franklin D. Roosevelt had to address the devastating unemployment of the Great Depression. One answer was creation of the Civilian Conservation Corps, later known as Roosevelt's "Tree Army," or simply the CCC, which put thousands of young men to work in the nation's parks, forests, and soil conservation districts.

The first CCC "boys" (ages 18 to 25) arrived in Shenandoah in May 1933 in army trucks, three years before its official dedication as a national park. The first two camps were established at Skyland and Big Meadows in that year, and in 1934 the number of camps had grown to six. Finally, it would reach 11 in and next to the park. As historian Reed Engle has observed, "Shenandoah National Park, long be-

fore it was born, was officially baptized by the Civilian Conservation Corps."

In August 1933, FDR and a press entourage toured the area and visited a CCC camp. Enrollees put on a skit in which they burned "Old Man Depression" in effigy to the bugler's tune of "Happy Days Are Here Again."

Dramatic presentations aside, the CCC in Shenandoah proved essential in readying the new park for the visiting public. A thousand recruits working at any one time built masonry walls along Skyline Drive, comfort stations, and drinking fountains. They surveyed land, planted hundreds of thousands of trees and shrubs, built picnic areas and campgrounds, fought fires, and rehabilitated cabins at Skyland with chestnut siding cut at a CCC saw-

mill. Some learned radio repair and other skills they could take with them when they returned home. For all CCCers, pay was $30 a month, most of which was sent back to their families.

It has been said that "if you build it, they will come." People did indeed begin arriving in Shenandoah, with plenty of opportunity to admire the handiwork of the CCC. In 1935 park visitation was about a half million; a mere two years later, the number topped one million, the first time a national park anywhere in the country reached that figure.

But the CCC would soon become a thing of the past. With the dawning of World War II and the military callup, all of Shenandoah's CCC camps closed. Each year alumni still come back to the park for a reunion.

ABOVE: Stone wall at Gooney Run Overlook. PHOTO ©MICHAEL COLLIER   **OPPOSITE:** Pool at Little Stony Man. PHOTO ©LAURENCE PARENT
PAGE 44/45: Sunrise, Buck Hollow Overlook. PHOTO ©CHARLES GURCHE

THE NATURAL WORLD

On a Sunday afternoon, leaden clouds hanging in the sky don't stop families from partaking of a picnic out on the rock observation platform on Hawksbill Mountain, the highest point in Shenandoah. An older couple, teasing each other like teenagers, eagerly points out their home in the valley below. Other hikers snap pictures and head back down the trail.

I find a flat rock and position myself for a good view, because Hawksbill is probably the best place in the park to spot a peregrine falcon. Information posted in the hiking shelter here tells of attempts to reintroduce these magnificent aerialists to the central Appalachians. Hawksbill, with its steep cliffs, is one of the sites where young peregrines are being released in an attempt to restore them to their native mountains.

In the 20th century, the use of DDT and other pesticides sounded the death knell for peregrines. After they ingested DDT, their eggshells thinned and shattered before the young could hatch, sending the population plummeting. As late as 1975, one naturalist wrote that the effects of pesticides had left the birds so vulnerable that "it is doubtful that peregrines will ever again nest on the cliffs of Shenandoah."

But with a ban on DDT and other pesticides in the United States, these birds of prey started to come back. After a 40-year absence from the Appalachians, peregrines were reintroduced successfully in Virginia; a pair nested in Shenandoah from 1994 to 1998 and raised chicks. But when the female failed to return, a program began in which "foster" peregrine chicks are brought from coastal areas and released each spring at "hack" sites on cliffs in the park. With minimal human contact, they are fed until they fledge and learn to hunt on their own.

Nearly half the birds have been implanted with transmitters, so their seasonal movements can be tracked. Some have gone south for the winter, while others, surprisingly, have headed to the northeast. As of 2004, however, none had returned to the hack sites in the park to nest. Despite discouraging news so far, biologists still hope to establish 21 breeding peregrine pairs in the central and southern Appalachians.

On this afternoon, I sit for some time with my eyes sharp and fingers crossed. But finally I must leave without seeing a falcon. Still, along with many others I too hold hope that a success story is in the making for one of our planet's species.

Another creature inhabits this part of the park too—the Shenandoah salamander, a lungless amphibian, reddish-brown in color and only two to four inches long. Every one of them known in the world lives only on the edges of rock slides on upper Hawksbill, Stony Man, and The Pinnacle in this park.

TOP
Northern copperhead in leaf litter.
PHOTO ©ADAM JONES
ABOVE
Red-shouldered hawk.
PHOTO ©WILLIAM B. FOLSOM

The Appalachian Mountains are a hotbed of salamander life. Some 14 species have been recorded in Shenandoah alone, and their diversity only increases to the south. The Shenandoah salamander is endangered, a plight owed more to a natural competitor than to a human one. The far more common red-backed salamander appears to be winning the contest for food and territory, forcing the Shenandoah salamander ever farther into a rocky corner. Odds are slim that I'll ever see a Shenandoah salamander, but as with peregrine falcons, just knowing they're here adds to the natural wonderment of this place.

Of course, I do see plenty of other creatures in the park—white-tailed deer, rufous-sided towhees, gray squirrels, wild turkeys, black rat snakes, a black bear. Shenandoah's 300 square miles harbor an embarrassment of biological riches. Some 2,000 species of plants and animals are known, and that doesn't count all the invertebrates, which could handily double that number. Two factors—elevation and precipitation—go a long way toward explaining this remarkable diversity. With elevation ranging from about 600 feet to more than 4,000 feet, the park presents a wide array of environments to animals and plants. Abundant precipitation, mostly rain and sometimes snow, averages about 50 inches a year. Fog and dew contribute too, watering a multilayered forest of trees, shrubs, flowers, ferns, mosses, and fungi.

Things were different in the 1920s, when the park was authorized. The land had been heavily used and only with protection did the forest begin to recover. First, bear oak and pitch pine started moving into the old fields and pastures, and a half century later classic forest succession was in evidence. Nearly all the park land now is cloaked with hardwoods like yellow poplar, oaks, and hickories. These broadleaf trees are a self-fulfilling prophesy—as their shade keeps the ground moister, and their yearly leaf fall pumps organic material into the soil, the environment becomes ever more conducive to their growth.

If the forest continued a steady march toward old age, it would only become richer in these and other species. But as in any ecosystem, change is no stranger to the forest. Disturbances such as fire, the attack of gypsy moths, and the downing of trees by wind and other natural causes, create openings or "light gaps" where pioneer species begin to recolonize.

Most of the trees in Shenandoah's forest are still less than a hundred years old, and awe-inspiring virgin specimens are hard to find. Still, on a gilded fall morning on a hike to South River Falls, I began to "feel" the change in the recovering forest. As the trail switchbacked down the mountainside, interesting ferns and intriguing mushrooms caught my eye. Dropping down into the headwaters of South River, where the flow from a spring coalesced into a stream, I sensed a subtle difference in the forest—the trees were bigger and of different kinds, with sugar maples and basswoods becoming more prominent, along with birches and eastern hemlocks on north-facing slopes and near the water. Enmeshed in its web spun between two tree trunks was an arachnid that I dubbed the "Halloween spider" for its psychedelic orange, yellow, and black markings.

On my way back up the trail after viewing the falls, I couldn't resist lingering by the stream, hypnotized by the twists and turns of the water, absent-mindedly arranging a mosaic of leaves of all shapes and colors—red, yellow, orange, brown. Deep in reverie, I started to see the patterns and orderliness of nature, the essential paradox of wild places. The word "sublime" came to mind, on a perfect October day in this always-living, every-changing place.

THE BIRDS

A glad chorus of bird song fills the air on Shenandoah mornings. More than 200 species of birds have been recorded in the park, avian variety that can be daunting for beginning birdwatchers struggling to graduate beyond the "little gray bird" and "little brown bird" stage. Patterns help. Time of day or time of year, type of habitat, and a bird's activity are useful to note. Is it early morning or evening, spring or fall, deep woods or open grasslands, low elevation or high? Is the bird flitting on the ground or flying in the canopy?

You'll know it's springtime in Shenandoah when you hear the American woodcock in early March, showing off at dusk over Big Meadows in whirling courtship flight. Also in spring before the trees fully leaf out, a wave of songbirds washes over the mountains—tanagers, vireos, warblers, swifts, swallows, and grosbeaks. Some will stay for about three months, building nests and giving birth. These neotropical migrants are the ones that must have seen the ads in the Sunday travel sections, wintering in Central and South America. Their return each year ushers in exuberant life and bright flashes of color to the woods.

In summer, the vibrant indigo bunting is unmistakable at overlooks along Skyline Drive. The red-eyed vireo is so common that it's often considered the signature bird of the eastern deciduous forest. Down on the ground, scratching in the leaf litter, is the rufous-sided towhee. A close look reveals its garnet-colored eye. The ruby-throated hummingbird, the only one of its kind that nests east of the Mississippi River, darts from flower to flower, sipping nectar.

Through summer the thick foliage of the trees renders most birds invisible, but not inaudible. Most, like the vociferous American goldfinch, are singing in the morning hours. A few, though, are strictly nocturnal—the wood thrush serenades on velvet summer evenings, while eastern screech owls, great-horned owls, and barred owls fill dark nights with their haunting calls. With the special feather anatomy of their wings, owls fly soundlessly in search of prey.

By later summer the warblers, vireos, and tanagers are readying for the trip south. To fuel their long-distance travels, they fatten on a succession of ripening berries of spicebush, sassafras, and dog

TOP
Male American goldfinch.
PHOTO ©ADAM JONES
MIDDLE
Blue jay.
PHOTO ©ADAM JONES
BOTTOM
Female northern cardinal.
PHOTO ©ADAM JONES

wood. By mid September, the urgency to depart grips the big raptors too. Hawks in particular attract attention, with the broad-winged hawk migration reaching a crescendo from September 15 to 25. Red-tailed hawks follow the ridgetops, searching for mice, rodents, birds, and snakes. Ravens, in black priestly shrouds, also fly in the highest mountains. They can be told from their crow cousins by their larger body and bill. Only a few birds stay through the winter, leaving the woods quiet except for the occasional Carolina chickadee caroling its chick-a-dee-dee-dee call.

Found at high elevations among red spruce and eastern hemlocks are northern birds such as the veery and solitary vireo. Dark-eyed juncos prefer the hemlocks, while the Blackburnian warbler is tied to them exclusively. A host of other warblers—Kentucky, black-throated green, black-and-white, and yellow-throated—flocks to old apple orchards. In fields and open grasslands, notably at Big Meadows, the gray catbird is a reliable summer resident. Meadowlarks, barn swallows, flycatchers, song sparrows, and other "prairie" birds can also be spotted there. Along streams a wood warbler known as the Louisiana waterthrush builds its nest, and belted kingfishers stand guard in tall trees.

Wild turkeys are a big comeback story for Shenandoah. They lost out to hunters and altered habitat, but were reintroduced after the park was established. The turkeys have done well for themselves, and today travelers are treated to large family flocks pecking at acorns and insects along Skyline Drive.

THE MAMMALS

Names of places in Shenandoah—Elkwallow and Wolf Run—speak of mammals that once inhabited this place. And though elk and wolves have been gone for some time, some 50 species of mammals are known here today, ranging in size from big black bears and white-tailed deer to tiny shrews and bats. Because of shared traits—warm-bloodedness, mammary glands, and hair—we humans tend to feel close kinship with other mammals.

The furred creatures most commonly seen in the park include deer, groundhogs, gray foxes, and eastern cottontails. But many, like opossums and raccoons, are nocturnal or secretive and not as readily observable. While waiting for that exciting sighting, it's always interesting to look closely for sign—burrows, tracks, scat, or claw marks.

The large mammal most visitors will get a close look at is the Virginia white-tailed deer, along Skyline Drive, in Big Meadows, at campgrounds, even walking tamely past a hiker on a trail. By the early 20th century, deer were almost entirely hunted out of what would become Shenandoah. But in 1934, the Mount Vernon Ladies Club donated 16 of them, which were released near Skyland. From that small nucleus the whitetail herd has expanded to perhaps several thousand animals, about as many as the range can support, according to biologists. Openings and edges in the second-growth forest are

TOP
Male indigo bunting. PHOTO ©ADAM JONES
MIDDLE
Eastern screech owl, red-phase.
PHOTO ©ADAM JONES
BOTTOM
Great horned owl.
PHOTO ©WILLIAM B. FOLSOM

ideal habitat for them, offering a bounty of preferred foods—leaves, flowers, twigs, buds, and grasses in spring and summer, and acorns and wild (and orchard) fruits in the fall. Fawns are born in early May and June, and their spotted coats keep them well camouflaged until they're able to stand on spindly legs. By the end of summer, deer molt their thin red-brown coats to winter's thicker buff-gray. By October, the bucks sport full racks of antlers, employed in fierce head-butting contests with other males to impress the does.

The top predator of deer is the mountain lion, also known as panther or cougar. This beautiful cat is mostly gone from the Appalachians and all the eastern United States now. But sightings are still reported, and mammalogists are keenly interested in confirming the presence of mountain lions. The other wild feline—the stub-tailed bobcat—is by all signs doing well in the park, finding plentiful rabbits and rodents to eat. Bobcat births peak about the same time as deer fawns; by September of the year, the young are weaned, but will stay with mom until they're about a year old. Once on their own, bobcats lead a mostly solitary existence over a large home range. They stay active most of the year, as do bats, mice, opossums, and raccoons.

It's the small things that really matter here though. The most abundant mammals in the park are likely deer mice and their brethren. Near the base of the food pyramid, their abundance forms an essential foundation for foxes and other carnivores.

The squirrel clan—groundhogs, gray squirrels, red squirrels, fox squirrels, and chipmunks—is well represented too. The rotund groundhog is often seen, especially along the shoulder of Skyline Drive. In the fall squirrels depend on the acorn crop, consuming some and caching others to carry them through winter. Red squirrels furiously guard their caches. Gray squirrels are picky eaters—they choose red oak acorns first, then those of chestnut oak and white oak. But none of the oaks reliably produce nuts every year. Populations of all the squirrels rise and fall with the nut crop. An unusual member of this group, the southern flying squirrel, doesn't actually fly but instead launches from trees and gains lift by spreading the cape of skin that extends from front to hind legs. This silken-furred creature needs mature trees or dead snags with cavities, mostly created by woodpeckers.

Some mammals are restricted by elevation and habitat needs. Denizens of higher elevations in Shenandoah include chattery red squirrels and diminutive red-backed voles. Beavers stay near water, usually at lower elevations. Bears favor the forest, and cottontails bound through meadows. Others, such as bobcats, striped skunks, and gray foxes are widely cosmopolitan in their ranges. And because of its geographic location, Shenandoah is a meeting ground for northern and southern species of mammals. Harvest mice and spotted skunks, rare here, may reach their northernmost limits, while the woodland jumping mouse and the masked shrew reach the southernmost extent of their ranges.

TOP
Groundhog (or woodchuck).
PHOTO ©ADAM JONES
TOP MIDDLE
Bobcat. PHOTO ©ADAM JONES
BOTTOM MIDDLE
Fox kits at den. PHOTO ©ADAM JONES
BOTTOM
White-tailed deer and fawn.
PHOTO ©PAT & CHUCK BLACKLEY

PAGE 52/53: Dogwoods in early-spring fog. PHOTO ©CARR CLIFTON

TOP
Lichen-covered boulder and foggy forest.
PHOTO ©CARR CLIFTON
BOTTOM
Ferns in autumn glory near Skyland.
PHOTO ©CARR CLIFTON

THE TREES

Shenandoah is possessed by trees. Ninety-five percent of the park's 300 square miles is forested. Along Skyline Drive and almost every trail and stream, trees are constant companions. Nearly all are deciduous, putting on a robe of breathtaking colors in autumn, dropping into winter dormancy, then unfurling a new growth of astonishing green in the spring. Trees reach for the sunlight, and like millions of little factories the leaves transform light and carbon dioxide into a crucial life-giving product—oxygen. For that service alone, we owe them undying thanks.

Some 100 species of trees, of both northern and southern heritage, find a meeting ground in the central Appalachians. Most trees have favored habitats, and they form distinct communities. On the park's lowest slopes and along streams rise the tulip trees. Also called tulip poplars or yellow poplars, they are in fact not related to poplars. Instead, the big yellow and orange flowers reveal their kinship to the magnolia. Often second-growth trees, yellow poplars fill in cut and grazed land, sometimes forming almost pure stands of straight-trunked trees.

A unique community of trees grows in the deep, moister soils of the mid elevations. Known as cove hardwoods, they include maple, birch, cherry, ash, and basswood. The wood of these trees is a cabinetmaker's dream. Pioneers tapped maple sap to make sugar, and ash was the chosen wood for tool handles. For the natural world, this forest type shelters an unparalleled diversity of life. Bees love the nectar of the basswood flower, and birds covet the fruits of the cherry trees.

Oaks, along with hickories and American chestnuts, once covered Shenandoah. The chestnut was prized for its tough wood and delicious nuts, relished both by bears and people. But in the early 20th century, the spores of a fungus introduced from Asia were blown in by the wind. Infected trees were killed in only a few years. By the 1930s, the American chestnut was gone from the entire eastern forest, an inestimable loss. The old stumps still send up sprouts, but the blight gets them before they can attain any size. Efforts to beat the blight and restore this invaluable tree are ongoing.

Today, the oaks and hickories are still supreme on the upper slopes and ridges—chestnut oak, red oak, and white oak, along with pignut hickory. White oaks can grow to 100 or 150 feet tall, and the round-lobed leaves distinguish them from other oaks. These nut-bearing trees are the larder for jays, turkeys, bears, and squirrels. From tiny acorns mighty oaks do grow, but many in this group also reproduce by sprouting. Beneath these stately trees grows an understory of smaller trees and shrubs—serviceberry, witch hazel, chokecherry, dogwood, and redbud—that can outshine their larger neighbors with gorgeous flower displays.

The evergreen eastern hemlocks drape delicate foliage over cool, moist, north-facing slopes. Groves of these massive, graceful elders have inspired visitors to the Limberlost area for a long time. Unfortunately, nearly all the hemlocks in Shenandoah have fallen victim to another invader, the hemlock wooly adelgid. These insects literally suck the lifeblood out of the trees, and in only 10 years they've left pale, barren destruction in their wake.

Pines, mostly pitch and Virginia pines, and black locust favor drier spots with thinner soils. They pioneer old fields and provide shade that hardwood seedlings need to grow. The hardwoods will eventually overtop the colonizing species.

Fossil pollen has revealed some fascinating stories about changes in the forest here over a longer term. From pollen, Ron Litwin and other researchers have been able to reconstruct the park's vegetation history over the past 45,000 years. With climate shifts, Litwin discovered frequent shifts in forest types, creating a complex mosaic. As recently as 22,000 years ago, when it was intensely cold, the park area was entirely conifer forest. But by 12,000 years ago, the Appalachian oak forest we see today had become established.

A few relics from the ice-age attic have survived at the highest elevations in the park. On Hawksbill Mountain, for example, red spruce and balsam fir still grow in the chill air, remnants of the boreal forest. Stunning large red spruces can be seen in the Limberlost area. Some of the fir, at least, were planted by the CCC, but others grow naturally. Also found in Limberlost is the only population of alder-leaved buckthorn known in Virginia. The buckthorn, along with gray birch in Big Meadows, reach their farthest southern limits here.

THE WILDFLOWERS

"Earth laughs in flowers," wrote Ralph Waldo Emerson. That laughter rings through the hills and hollows of Shenandoah in spring and summer. It would take an entire book to feature all the wildflowers in the park—862 species at latest count—so we highlight only a few standouts in this all-star cast.

Just as migrating songbirds wash over the mountains in early spring, so do blooming wildflowers, sweeping from the valleys up the mountainsides. The earliest arrival is the odd-looking skunk cabbage. Though not the most beautiful of flowers, it's no less welcome when it peeks above thawing ground in early or mid February. In March, the real show begins with the appearance of bloodroot, bluets, and trailing arbutus. The well-named spring beauty shyly hugs the ground in vernal purity. And there's smoky-pink hepatica, another harbinger of spring, which was to naturalist John Burroughs "the gem of the woods."

From April into May, it's a cast of thousands: bellwort, blazing star, bleeding heart, buttercup, Dutchman's breeches, Solomon's seal, violets, and mayapples, their white flowers hiding beneath huge parasol leaves. Colors grow bolder—yellows, reds, and purples—and the flowers are best seen on lower slopes and in the coves. Most are spring ephemerals, those that bloom before the trees leaf out and while the soil is still cool and moist. They flower and set fruit in only about two months, and then

TOP
Turkey-tail fungus.
PHOTO ©FRED HIRSCHMANN
MIDDLE
Mustards and spiderwort.
PHOTO ©WILLARD CLAY
BOTTOM
Wild geraniums.
PHOTO ©WILLARD CLAY

vanish.

Take the trail to Hightop in early May for a grand show of trilliums. A singular large flower, most often white or regal crimson, tops each stem. The trillium's three-part anatomy tells of kinship with the lilies. Also known by the common name wake robin, several species, including the exquisite painted trillium, can be found in Shenandoah.

Also through the month come wild columbines and geraniums, foamflowers, cinquefoil, and the captivating lady's-slipper orchids, both yellow and pink forms. The park boasts some 18 species of orchids, with rare beauties among them like the small whorled pogonia and large purple-fringed. For insects, orchids can be a house of horrors, but the plants are merely employing sophisticated methods to assure continuation of their kind. Insects are drawn by the sweet fragrance, and once inside they fall prey to deceiving "traps" and "mirrors" that hold them until they've picked up pollen to be deposited on another flower of the species.

Growing deep in the cove hardwood forest in April and May is a most unusual plant, Jack-in-the-pulpit. No stereotypical wildflower, this member of the arum family is wonderfully strange. A fleshy stalk stands beneath a greenish, striped hood. "Jack" huddles in perfect camouflage in the shaded woodland; when the clump of shocking red fruits appears in fall, though, the plant is hard to miss.

But don't leave yet. Arriving on stage later in May are the Appalachian specialties, mountain laurel and rhododendron. Into June these shrubs of the heath family erupt in breathtaking shades of pink, rose, purple, and white. The gorgeous flowers of mountain laurel are like finely painted porcelain. The stamens are tucked tightly into pockets in the petals. When the flower fully opens, it does so with a flourish, releasing those spring-loaded stamens and their pollen to the universe. Mountain azalea (a rhododendron) offers a sweet scent and deep-pink blooms. It's a real stage-stopper along the Stony Man Trail.

By early June, the canopy of trees blocks most sunlight from the forest floor. Still, a few leggier flowers do bloom through summer—bellflowers, beebalm, and Turk's-cap lilies among them. In the fall goldenrods, gentians, purple asters, and Deptford pinks decorate the roadside, while spotted jewelweed and cardinal flower adorn streambanks and moist ravines. These remaining flowers draw monarch butterflies, thousands of them stopping each day to sip nectar to power their marathon trips to wintering grounds, mostly in Mexico. Every monarch generation returns to the same roosts in the Sierra Madre, some even to the same trees. They could not do so without the aid of flowers. With the exit of these last blossoms, the curtain falls on Shenandoah's lavish floral performance for another year.

In mid May each year, visitors can join Shenandoah's Wildflower Weekend, which celebrates the incredible display with hikes, talks, and ranger programs. Also, a stroll on almost any park trail will lead into this garden of botanical delights.

BEARS

Biologists estimate there may be one bear every square mile in Shenandoah National Park, the greatest density of these animals anywhere in North America.

The black bear—*Ursus americanus*—has made a remarkable comeback here. In the 1930s, two bears were reintroduced to the national park. Protected there, through the 1940s and 1950s their numbers had reached about 30. By the early 1990s, bear numbers had multiplied tenfold, to about 300.

Bears are animals of the deep woods, and often will vanish up a tree if they see—or more likely smell—humans. Yet in the park, it's not uncommon to see them eating grubs along Skyline Drive or picking apples in developed areas, paying little attention to people's presence.

In summer, black bears are out beating the bushes for food. Omnivores, they will eat nearly anything—bugs, berries, nuts, even small mammals and carrion. In September and October, they are in a true feeding frenzy, gorging on acorns and hickory nuts, putting on three to five pounds a day, mostly as fat to carry them through long winter days and nights. Though bears aren't true hibernators, they spend three to four months in dens, usually rock cavities or hollow trees. They do not eat, drink, or eliminate any wastes during this time. Females give birth and nurse cubs in the dens as well. By mid April the males, and then the females with young, arise and venture out.

At this time they suffer from a real "nutritional deficit," says bear researcher Michael Vaughn, gobbling anything and everything. They survive on grasses and roots until the bounty of summer and fall is again available. This is also when mom kicks out her young from the previous year, and when visitors might see these solitary bears as they begin staking out their own territories.

Bears will wander. Shenandoah's lengthy, irregular boundary bumps up against farms and orchards that naturally draw bears to apples and honey. It's a setup for potential conflicts. Bears that go onto private lands are subject to legal hunting in season. Game officials may relocate some that stray, but bears have a strong homing instinct and will usually find their way back to the park. Poachers kill bears merely for their gall bladders or paws, illegally sold on a thriving international black market.

What bears don't need is a handout. "A fed bear is a dead bear" is more than a catchy slogan—it is fact. Park visitors are cautioned to keep all food out of sight in vehicles, hung from a high limb in the backcountry, and never taken into the tent or left out on the picnic table.

ABOVE: Black bear cub. PHOTO ©ADAM JONES

THREATS TO THE FOREST

The spirit-lifting views from Skyline Drive in Shenandoah are a source of awe—most of the time. Sadly, those vistas have been clouded by diminished air quality. The once-stunning visibility is suffering from a buildup of haze from sources other than the natural products released during plant photosynthesis.

Some of the murkiness arises from sulfate particles from the smokestacks of power plants as far away as the Ohio River Valley. Visibility has been reduced from an estimated 115 miles to fewer than 25 miles on average. In summer it is even worse, shrinking to only a mile on bad days. Shenandoah ranks as third worst among national parks that monitor visibility.

Another air-related threat, albeit less visible, comes from acid deposition—from wet sources such as rain, snow, and fog, and from dry sources as well.

Again, the culprits are sulfur dioxide and nitrogen oxide emitted mostly from power plants. Though the park's high-elevation streams are naturally acidic, as that level rises the rare brook trout and other forms of aquatic life are jeopardized. Increased acidity in soils also damages tree roots. Ozone is a growing problem, and symptoms such as damaged leaves, early leaf drop, and slowed growth have been witnessed in some plants. A problem city dwellers hope to escape is now following them up into the mountains.

Meanwhile, park biologists are taking aim against invasive exotic plants and animals. Often, these non-native species can outcompete the natives. The entry of coyotes into the park may prove a problem for bobcats, but coyotes aren't being removed because they fill a predator niche resulting from the absence of wolves. Introduced brown and rainbow

trout threaten native brook trout; they've been known to interbreed and produce hybrids such as the tiger trout. Intruding insects have also wreaked devastation in the forest—gypsy moth caterpillars on oaks and wooly adelgids on the park's great stands of eastern hemlocks. Many of the 300 non-native plants documented in the park need to be reined in—among them the tree-of-heaven, Oriental bittersweet, and Japanese honeysuckle.

Problems of air pollution and non-native plants and insects have led to Shenandoah's designation as one of the country's "Top Ten" most endangered national parks by the National Parks Conservation Association. Hope of removing Shenandoah from this list will take the best efforts of everyone who cares for this special place.

ABOVE: Brown Mountain. PHOTO ©TIM FITZHARRIS

OPPOSITE: Azaleas and ferns at the edge of the forest. PHOTO ©FRED HIRSCHMANN

PAGE 60/61: Virginia pine and the Shenandoah Valley. PHOTO ©CARR CLIFTON

RESOURCES AND INFORMATION

EMERGENCY & MEDICAL
Dial 911, or (800) 732-0911

FOR MORE INFORMATION
National Parks on the Internet
www.nps.gov
Shenandoah National Park
3655 U.S. Highway 211 East
Luray, VA 22835
(540) 999-3500 (Visitor Information Recorded Message)
www.nps.gov/shen
Shenandoah National Park Association
3655 U.S. Highway 211 East
Luray, VA 22835
(540) 999-3582
www.snpbooks.org
Appalachian Trail Project Office
National Park Service
Harpers Ferry, WV 25425

For official Appalachian Trail Guides and maps, contact:
Appalachian Trail Conference
P.O. Box 807
Harpers Ferry, WV 25425
(304) 535-6331, or 888-AT-STORE

CAMPING INSIDE THE PARK
Phone (800) 365-CAMP (2267) for reservations at Big Meadows and Dundo Group Campground.
On the Internet:
www.reservations.nps.gov.

BACKCOUNTRY CABIN RENTALS
Potomac Appalachian Trail Club
118 Park Street, SE
Vienna, VA 22180
(703) 242-0693
www.pate.net

LODGING INSIDE THE PARK
ARAMARK
P.O. Box 727
Luray, VA 22835
Toll-free (800) 999-4714,
or locally (540) 743-5108
Web Site: www.visitshenandoah.com

LODGING OUTSIDE THE PARK
Front Royal Visitor Center
414 East Main Street
Front Royal, VA 22630
(800) 338-2576 or (540) 635-5788
www.ci.front-royal.va.us
Luray-Page County Chamber of Commerce
46 East Main Street
Luray, VA 22835
(540) 743-3915
www.luraypage.com
Waynesboro Tourism Office
301 West Main Street
Waynesboro, VA 22980
Toll Free (866) 253-1957, or (540) 942-6644
www.waynesboro.va.us
Charlottesville/Albemarle Convention & Visitor Bureau
600 College Drive
Charlottesville, VA 22902
(434) 977-1783
www.charlottesvilletourism.org

Shenandoah Valley Travel Association
P.O. Box 1040
New Market, VA 22844
(540) 740-3132
www.shenandoah.org

CAMPING OUTSIDE THE PARK
George Washington and **Jefferson National Forests**
112 North River Road
Bridgewater, VA
(540) 828-2591
www.southernregion.fs.fed.us/gw
Virginia State Parks Reservation Center
(800) 933-PARK
www.dcr.state.va.us

OTHER REGIONAL SITES
Blue Ridge Parkway
199 Hemphill Knob Road
Asheville, NC 28803
(828) 271-4779
www.nps.gov/blri
Luray Caverns
U.S. Highway 211 Bypass
Luray, VA 22835
(540) 743-6551
www.luraycaverns.com
Monticello
Virginia Route 53
Charlottesville, VA
(434) 984-9822
www.monticello.org
Virginia Civil War Trails
Virginia Tourism Commission
(888) CIVIL WAR (248-4592)
www.civilwar-va.com

ABOVE: White-tailed deer in Big Meadows. PHOTO ©JERRY L. WHALEY

SUGGESTED READING

Amberson, Joanne. *Hikes to Peaks & Vistas, Hikes to Waterfalls, and Short Hikes.* Booklet series, Shenandoah National Park Association, Luray, VA. 2002.

Badger, Robert L. *Geology Along Skyline Drive: A Self-Guided Tour for Motorists.* Shenandoah National Park Association, Luray, VA. 1999.

Crandall, Hugh and Reed Engle. *Shenandoah: The Story Behind the Scenery.* KC Publications, Las Vegas. Revised edition, 1997.

Engle, Reed L. *In The Light of the Mountain Moon: An Illustrated History of Skyland.* Shenandoah National Park Association, Luray, VA. 2003.

Engle, Reed L. *Everything Was Wonderful: A Pictorial History of the CCC in Shenandoah National Park.* Shenandoah National Park Association, Luray, VA. 1998.

Gathright, Thomas M. II. *Geology of the Shenandoah National Park, Virginia.* Bulletin 86, Virginia Division of Mineral Resources, Charlottesville. Reprint 2003.

Horning, Audrey. *In the Shadow of Ragged Mountain: Historical Archaeology of Nicholson, Corbin and Weakley Hollows.* Shenandoah National Park Association, Luray, VA. 2004.

Lambert, Darwin. *The Undying Past of Shenandoah National Park.* Reinhart Books and Shenandoah Natural History Association. 1989.

Lindsay, Terry and Patressa Lindsay. *Birds of Shenandoah National Park.* Shenandoah Natural History Association. Luray, VA. 1997.

Redfern, Ron. *Origins: The Evolution of Continents, Oceans, and Life.* University of Oklahoma Press, Norman. 2001.

Skyline Drive: An Audio Driving Tour. Shenandoah National Park Association, 2003.

ABOVE: Falls on Hogcamp Branch, autumn. PHOTO ©PAT & CHUCK BLACKLEY

PRODUCTION CREDITS

Publisher: Jeff D. Nicholas
Author: Rose Houk
Editor: Nicky Leach
Illustrations: Darlece Cleveland
Printing Coordination: Tien Wah Press

ISBN 1-58071-062-X (Paper)
ISBN 13: 9781-58071 062-6
©2006 Sierra Press

Printed in the Republic of South Korea.
First printing, Spring 2006.

SIERRA PRESS
4988 Gold Leaf Drive
Mariposa, CA 95338
e-mail: siepress@sti.net

www.NationalParksUSA.com

OPPOSITE
Skyline Drive north of Swift Run Gap, autumn.
PHOTO ©PAT & CHUCK BLACKLEY